Linda Waniorek

Fitness Planner for Your Dog

Photos by Christine Steimer

Illustrations by György Jankovics

CONTENTS

THAT'S A TYPICAL DOG!

- Enjoys life and is an active partner for its owner.

- Needs plenty of physical exercise and activity.

- Is always ready for fun and games.

- Seeks contact with other members of its species.

- Can keep physically fit even in old age.

- Loves to be near its owner and adapts to his or her wishes.

- Is a good companion and guardian for the entire family.

For many thousands of years, dogs have served humans as companions and helpers, performing their duties with energy, tenacity, and devotion to their owners. In earlier times, those duties centered around assisting hunters and herding livestock, as well as guarding house and home and loved ones. As a result of those continual requirements, dogs have retained many of the genetic traits they inherited from their ancestor, the wolf: obedience to a higher-ranking individual, and a powerful need for physical activity. Today, however, dogs are usually not kept for work, but for the pleasure of their owners and as a means of warding off loneliness. In many cases, the result is a clear lack of exercise and activity. As a result, health problems appear in increasing numbers, and the dog's quality of life diminishes. The best remedy is a well-planned fitness program tailored to the dog's specific needs.

THE RULES OF FITNESS

1 Before any sports activity, always give your dog a chance to get warmed up. Let your pet run around for a few minutes before you start the exercise session. Then begin the exercises slowly, then gradually increase their intensity.

2 Never let your dog exercise with a full stomach; the result could be a dangerous gastric torsion, or twisting of the stomach (see TIP, page 23).

3 Increase the exercise demands on your pet steadily, but slowly, so that the dog is not overtaxed.

4 Keep in mind the capabilities of your dog's breed; that is the only way your pet can achieve its "personal best."

5 Adapt sports and games to the individual abilities and talents of your dog, as well as to its age. Otherwise, small breeds, puppies, and older animals in particular can be easily overtaxed.

6 In training, also take into account any health impairments your dog may have. Always discuss the dog's particular situation with your veterinarian ahead of time.

7 During sports, games, and training sessions, be lavish with your praise, and stroke your dog when it has done well—that's the only way to keep your pet motivated.

8 Never exercise your dog for a prolonged period in the blazing sun, especially not at noontime, because heatstroke may easily result. Instead, find shady spots for your activities.

9 During the session, give your pet plenty of breaks, so that it doesn't overdo and lose its interest in physical activity.

10 Make sure that your dog has a chance to drink plenty of water when it is physically active. After drinking, the dog needs to have a short break as well.

Dogs have an extremely strong need for physical activity, and for that very reason they take great pleasure in sports and games. A varied training program that includes plenty of spontaneous fun not only will give your pet more zest and a better quality of life, but also will keep it physically and mentally healthy and active well into advanced age. There will be no hint of boredom and lethargy, and behavioral problems will be rare if the dog's basic requirements for exercise and companionship with its owner and with other dogs are being met.

Regular exercise sessions to keep your dog fit are an ideal foundation for a satisfactory partnership between owner and pet.

HOW TO KEEP YOUR DOG FIT ALL YEAR

You can do a great deal to keep your dog fit. Exercise and a healthy diet are important if you want your pet to stay in good shape year-round, but proper grooming and use of gentle, natural remedies can also promote well-being and fitness.

Fitness Is More Than Just Exercise

Dogs need to be physically active. They need plenty of space to run around in, activities that are appropriate for their particular constitution, and little "jobs" that they can perform for their owner with a sense of duty and care. Only then will they be our agreeable, happy partners in every situation in life. A fitness program that includes its fair share of play will help fulfill all of those requirements. You will enjoy it as well—alone with your dog, together with other dog owners, or in one of the many dog sports clubs.

Space and opportunities for fun and games are available everywhere—whether in your home, in the city, or in natural surroundings. The change of the seasons, too, provides a variety of interesting opportunities for training (see Fitness Calendar, page 30). But fitness means more than just a little exercise.

Health: This is the basic prerequisite for a good physical condition and agility, and a well-designed training program can have a positive influence on many health problems. Lack of fit-ness, on the other hand, can substantially impair your dog's well-being, make it more susceptible to disease, and lower its average life expectancy. Adequate exercise and regular participation in sports and games with your pet, as well as preventive health care, are the best ways you can contribute to your dog's health and quality of life. Therapeutic massage and stretching exercises (see pages 19 and 20), as well as treatment with gentle, natural remedies (see page 18), are excellent ways of supporting the training program.

A balanced diet. Anyone who expends energy has to eat properly. Overweight and an unbalanced diet loaded with fat are detrimental to your pet's health. Only a well-balanced, healthful diet will promote your dog's well-being and increase its level of fitness (see page 22).

Regular grooming. Your dog will truly enjoy sports and games only when it feels like a million dollars. Overly long nails and parasites such as fleas and ticks can seriously impair its well-being and its enjoyment of physical activity. Therefore, grooming is an important part of any fitness program (see page 24).

Jogging with your dog is fun, and it will keep pet and owner equally fit.

Does Your Dog Need a Fitness Program?

Many dog owners ask themselves that question. Basically, the answer is that a training program makes sense for every dog.

Lack of fitness. An overweight dog's poor condition is visible even from a distance. The signs of a lack of fitness are not always so clear, however. Usually, easily overlooked behavioral signs are the first indication that your dog is in serious need of a fitness program:

✔ Your otherwise healthy dog seems indifferent to what is going on around it, often just lies around, and is reluctant to leave the place where it sleeps. When you walk around in the house, it doesn't follow.

✔ On walks, the dog trots slowly and listlessly behind you. It always takes the shortest way, and wants to go home early.

✔ Even after brief physical effort, the otherwise healthy dog is exhausted. It pants and needs a long time to recover.

When There's a Lack of Activity

Dogs that lack the opportunity or the incentive to move around freely and extensively or to help their owner "work" often have an especially poor constitution.

✔ In town, many dogs are kept almost exclusively indoors and are taken on only a few short walks, at most. Frequently there is no outdoor area where they can play, and thus they always have to be kept on their leash.

✔ Often, a dog's owner works and is away from home every day for many hours on end. Dogs that are left alone easily become bored.

✔ Dogs that are kept in a kennel, too, often get far too little exercise.

Start Carefully

The test on page 11 will help you decide whether and how urgently your dog needs a fitness program. If your pet is not fit, be sure not to overtax it, especially at the beginning. Work on getting the dog in shape slowly, but steadily. As its condition improves, you can ask more of your pet, and gradually expand the exercise program.

If your dog is in very poor shape, discuss the proposed training plan with a veterinarian before you start. He or she can diagnose health problems, if any, and suggest possible sources of help for your training program (see Information, page 60).

A tunnel will wake up your dog's "nose." It's especially nice if your pet finds you waiting at the other end.

TEST: Does Your Dog Need a Fitness Program?

Is Your Dog Fit?	Yes	No
1. Does your dog react with hesitation when you want to go for a walk?		
2. Does it have trouble getting up?		
3. Does it have a hard time climbing stairs?		
4. On walks, does it trot along tiredly and listlessly behind you?		
5. Does it take every opportunity to lie down?		
6. Does it avoid playing with other dogs?		
7. Is it reluctant to join you in a game?		
8. Does it stay in its place when you come home?		
9. Does it bark without leaving its place when the doorbell rings?		
10. Is it reluctant to leave the house?		
11. Is it overweight? (Keep breed-related variations in mind.)		
12. Does it pant constantly, and is its heartbeat rapid?		
13. Does it often lie around apathetically?		

✔ If you've answered "no" to all the questions, your dog is fit. Keep on providing it with plenty of exercise. This book will suggest many ways to do just that.

✔ If you've answered "yes" to any of the questions, it would be a good idea to help your pet get in better shape (see Sports and Games, page 12), but first have your pet checked out by your veterinarian to be sure no other health problems exist.

Sports and Games

Sports and games will not only give your dog a great deal of pleasure, but will also contribute substantially to a long, healthy life.

What to Keep in Mind

There's a suitable sport for every dog, but not every sport is right for all dogs. Your pet's age, breed, and state of health are the determining factors here. Before you involve your pet in an activity, find out about the animal's special strengths and weaknesses, and arrange for a thorough checkup by a veterinarian.

Breed-related limitations. High jumps, stair climbing, and obstacle races are not suit-

The slalom course is difficult, and your dog will need practice before negotiating it successfully.

able for small breeds, especially those with an elongated body, and for puppies of any breed.

No overexertion. Not every dog is inherently fit. Frequently, it takes a great deal of effort to get in shape. To prevent injury, however, you should avoid overly taxing activities and repetitive stress.

Motivation through communication. In the relationship between owner and dog, obedience often continues to come first. People disregard the fact that dogs are sensitive creatures that long for contact and do many things only out of love for their owner. In any fitness program, therefore, communication is of great importance. If you use kind words and a loving touch to encourage your dog to participate in sports, it generally will obey your wishes gladly.

Sports in a Club

Today, dog sports clubs offer more and more types of sports that promote fitness for pet and owner alike. Since individual facilities employ different methods, before joining a dog sports club you should make absolutely certain that your ideas about dealing with the dog and about training dogs in general are accepted there.

Agility will keep both dog and owner in shape. In this sport, the dog is supposed to negotiate an obstacle course as swiftly and with as few mistakes as possible. The owner runs alongside his pet, but is not allowed to touch the dog. Before a dog can perform tasks of this kind successfully, good obedience training and plenty of practice are necessary. For small breeds, there are special Agility courses.

Team dance, developed by Ekard Lind, is a relatively new kind of sport, based on pedagogical principles. It emphasizes harmonious communication between owner and pet, as well as treatment of the dog as a partner. Team dance offers numerous ways of linking sports and music in a mutual dance involving owner and dog. This sport is especially recommended for dog owners who like music and enjoy moving in time to music.

In flyball, the dog jumps over a series of hurdles and uses its paw to activate a ball-tossing machine. The dog catches the ball and, clearing the hurdles again, returns it as quickly as possible to its owner.

Checklist
What to Keep in Mind in Sports and Games

1 If your dog is inexperienced, restrict your activities to places where there are few distractions.

2 Make it a hard-and-fast rule to avoid repetitive stress; vary the training.

3 When training puppies and older dogs, take frequent breaks.

4 Never let your dog swim in water where the current is strong.

5 Never train your dog in quarries or on gravel-covered slopes; it could be injured.

6 Don't have your dog retrieve rocks; that could harm its teeth.

7 When biking with your dog— especially if it is small—always make sure to adjust your speed to its physical condition.

TIP

How Older Owners Can Keep Their Dogs Fit

As an older person, you may not always find it easy to give your dog the kind of fitness program it needs. Therefore, try to choose games in which your pet has to be as active as possible (such as retrieving). Be sure to provide good obedience training, so that you can let your pet off its leash.

A dog can easily be included in many athletic activities for older people. Several short walks each day will give your pet ample exercise. If possible, take the dog along whenever you leave home, and don't overlook opportunities for indoor activity (see HOW-TO: Winter Fitness, pages 58 and 59). If you're no longer able to give your dog enough exercise, it's a good idea to hire a dog walker to walk it on a regular basis.

Obedience is a sport that stresses obedience above all else. The dog has to follow its owner's directions, even from a considerable distance and despite all distractions.

Tournament sports include four disciplines: obedience, slalom course, obstacle course, and cross-country race.

Prerequisite for Dog Sports

Basic obedience training for your pet at a good dog school is a fine idea in any case, and it will create an ideal basis for your dog's subsequent training in a dog sports club. Contact addresses are available from the American Kennel Club (see Information, page 60).

Puppy classes. You should start developing the right basis for training as early as 12 weeks of age. Ideal for this purpose are "puppy play days," when the young dog learns, through play, to hold its own among other dogs of its age and to establish social contact. The play groups should include no more than 10 puppies.

Companion Dog test. From the age of 12 months on, your dog can take the Companion Dog test. In addition to obedience exercises (such as heeling while off the leash), it will learn to move safely in street traffic. Obedience and mastery of commands are major prerequisites for participation in a dog sports club.

Schutzhund training. This focuses on teaching the dog to obey, is very expensive and usually unnecessary for privately owned dogs.

In general, any kind of training for a dog makes sense only if

✔ no spiked collars or choke collars are in use.

✔ commands are given in a low voice.

✔ no force is applied.

✔ the dogs in the course all have roughly the same level of training.

✔ the course has no more than 10 participants.

Far too often, dogs are quite deliberately trained to be aggressive. Such dangerous practices are to be condemned in any case.

In addition to the courses mentioned above, there are special types of training for herd dogs, sled dogs, and hunting dogs. Bear in mind, however, that the dog has to have a chance to practice what it has learned after the course is over. If that is impossible, you should choose a different outlet for its need for physical exercise.

Sports and Games Without a Club

Even without participation in a club, your dog can keep in good shape. Whether on your own or in the company of others, you can involve your pet in games and sports almost everywhere, with little expense.

✔ The easiest solution is to have your dog accompany you as you jog, bike, or hike.

✔ On walks, you'll meet other dog owners. By playing with other members of its species, your pet can unleash its energy and exercise its entire body.

✔ You can use games for yourself and your pet to make the "walk around the house" into an effective fitness course. Dogs love all kinds of games involving running, catching, fetching, and tugging. You'll find a wide variety of suitable toys in any pet store.

Important: Even if you train your dog alone, rather than in a club, make sure you don't ask too much of your pet. In addition, always adapt the activity to the dog's level of physical fitness. Not all dogs are equal in ability, particularly when the sport requires intensive effort.

In endurance sports such as jogging and biking, medium- to large-sized breeds (such as German Shepherds, Dalmatians, retrievers, and Greyhounds) do

best. Small breeds, too, benefit from such endurance sports, but make sure you don't overtax your pet.

Swimming is great fun for most dogs. Golden Retrievers and Labrador Retrievers, as well as Newfoundlands, are real water lovers.

Winter sports are a good choice for medium-sized dogs with a dense coat—such as Huskies, Samoyeds, and German Shepherds—that don't get cold too easily and don't find running in relatively deep snow too strenuous.

In the chapters dealing with the individual seasons, you'll find a great many other suggestions for keeping your dog fit 12 months a year.

Dogs enjoy jumping over hurdles.

BEHAVIOR: AN INTERPRETER

Your dog can communicate with you through the sounds it makes and through its body language.

My dog displays this behavior.

What does my dog mean by this?

This is the right way for me to react to its behavior!

On its own, the dog jumps through the tire.

It enjoys sports and games.

Make s▯ you don't o▯ tax your pe▯

The dog is
visibly exhausted.

It is
overweight.

Start an easy fitness
program, but have it
checked by a veterinar-
ian first.

The dog brings you the Frisbee.

It wants to keep playing.

Throw the disk again.

Two puppies tussle.

While playing, they find out what their capabilities are.

Give your pet plenty of opp▯ tunities to play with other pupp▯

The dog digs a hole.

It scents something exciting.

Let your pet dig only where it can do no harm.

The dog looks at you expectantly.

It is inviting you to play.

Take this opportunity to work on your pet's fitness.

The dog howls.

It is bored.

Keep it occupied with sports and games.

The dog is supposed to go up ramp.

It's reluctant to do something familiar.

You can sweeten the pot by ring your pet a treat.

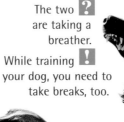

The big dog yawns.

The two are taking a breather.

While training your dog, you need to take breaks, too.

Your Dog's Health

Health and fitness go hand in hand. Only a dog that is in good condition has adequate resistance and a long life expectancy.

Holistic Treatment Methods

Essential oils and gentle natural remedies are good for prevention and treatment of minor complaints. If your dog has health problems, however, always consult a veterinarian.

Aromatherapy. The specific goals of this method of treatment are emotional balance, activation of the circulatory system, and strengthening of resistance. As with aromatherapy for humans, the essential oils are used in a scent lamp (let the lamp burn at least one hour) or an herbal pillow. Alternatively, they can be dripped directly onto the dog's sleeping area or mixed with products appropriate for dogs, such as shampoos (four to five drops). Never apply them directly to the dog, since they could irritate

*Massage strengthens the
muscles in a dog's back
and releases tension.*

its sensitive mucous membranes. The only exception is tea tree oil, which can be applied sparingly (one or two drops) to small injuries in order to disinfect them.

For information about which oils are especially good for dogs in which situations, see the sections on the individual seasons (pages 33, 40, 49, and 54).

Bach flower therapy is always in order when a dog is behaving strangely, is fearful or aggressive, barks a great deal, or forgets its toilet training. Bach flower remedies are available from many veterinarians, nonmedical practitioners, and pharmacies. Since each "case" is different, the Bach flowers have to be specifically selected by an expert, with your pet's particular situation in mind. For acute cases, so-called Rescue Drops or Rescue Ointments are available. Place two or three drops of the Bach flower remedy directly on the dog's tongue, or add that amount to its food. For minor injuries or sunburn, apply the ointment to the affected areas.

Homeopathy. To build up your pet's resistance and to treat chronic ailments, you can also use homeopathic remedies. These ingredients are time-tested: belladonna (muscle relaxant), bryony, cinchona, or Peruvian bark (states of exhaustion), cimicifuga or rattle root (pain in the joints and in the neck muscles), crataegus (circulatory problems), dulcamara (pain in the locomotor system), echinacea (strengthens resistance), hypericum (stress, anxiety), ignatia (stress, homesickness), pulsatilla (colds, anxiety), rhus toxicodendron (muscle cramps, exhaustion), ruta graveolens (overexertion, strained sinews). Homeopathic remedies are

Health Problems and Ways to Treat Them

Health Problems	Management in the Course of the Fitness Program
The neck and throat muscles are poorly developed or taut	Stretch the muscles in the head and neck area; have the dog retrieve sticks that you throw
The back is painfully twisted (the dog has trouble getting to its feet) or tense	Massage back cautiously along the spinal column; if no relief, seek veterinary assistance
The musculature is poorly developed in general	Encourage swimming; perform full-body massage
The hind legs won't bear much weight and give easily (the dog has trouble jumping)	Encourage swimming; stretch and massage hind legs; if overly painful, seek veterinary assistance
The dog has heart and circulatory problems (breathing heavily, panting, and/or a pulse that is clearly visible in the lower chest or neck region)	Seek veterinary assistance at once to rule out heart disease, heartworm disease, etc. Aromatherapy, Bach Rescue Drops, and homeopathic remedies may be used in conjunction with conventional veterinary medical treatments
The dog tires extremely rapidly	Seek veterinary assistance to rule out heart disease, hypothyroidism, etc.; if otherwise healthy, full-body massage and stretching may be used; encourage swimming

*If you suspect that your dog is suffering from a medical condition, always consult your veterinarian before beginning any type of treatment.

available in pharmacies. Especially suitable for dogs are strobuli (pellets): Place five to eight pellets in the side of the dog's mouth or in its throat, and stroke its neck to activate the swallowing reflex. Before using them, consult your veterinarian.

Massage and Stretching

Muscle stretching exercises (see page 20) and massage are not only good for you, they will help your dog as well, by releasing tension and stimulating blood circulation. Moreover, massage—provided your veterinarian approves—is also therapeutic, for example, as follow-up treatment of injuries or in cases of osteoarthritis.

How to massage. Talk to your dog quietly, and get it to lie down on its side or its belly. Start by gently stroking your pet all over. Then, slowly work toward the area that you plan to massage:

✔ Increasing the pressure, keep stroking the dog gently with the flat of your palm (stroking massage, or effleurage).

✔ Massage the dog with your fingers, making sure the pressure is not too strong (finger massage).

✔ Using both hands, take hold of the dog's skin and the tissue beneath, and knead it thoroughly, increasing the pressure from gentle to vigorous (kneading massage, or petrissage).

✔ With your fingertips, make circular movements (fingertip massage).

Important: A massage should last about 15 to 20 minutes, or less at first while you are getting your pet used to the procedure. Never massage your dog right after it has eaten or when it is exhausted.

Massage for specific areas of the body.

✔ When your dog obviously has pain in the head and neck area, a stroking massage of the head and neck is especially good for relieving tension, or just for creating a sense of closeness.

✔ A kneading or stroking massage of the shoulder area and front

Preventive health care is a prerequisite for a successful fitness program.

legs will help to develop muscles or relieve tension.

✔ For respiratory and circulatory problems—if your dog breathes heavily and pants a great deal, and these symptoms persist—as well as stomachache and gas pains, take your dog to your veterinarian immediately.

✔ Kneading and stroking massage focused on the hip and hind leg area can be helpful for dogs with hip dysplasia and osteoarthritis.

✔ Careful massage of the spinal area of a dog with taut muscles or osteoarthritis can have a positive effect on its state of health.

Stretching. Through gentle but continual training, muscles become stronger and more fully defined. Flexibility can be maintained with stretching exercises, which extend the muscles. To do the exercises, however, your pet needs your active participation. By extending and flexing various joints on the dog's body with your hands, you move it as if it were doing stretching exercises of its own accord. If you can clearly feel that your dog's neck muscles, for example, are stiff and tight, then place your palm on its head and press down until you detect a distinct counterpressure, then release. Do this about 10 to 20 times. This stretching exercise can be repeated several times a day, and it can be used for other parts of the body as well, such as the legs, back, and hips. For the legs, carefully pull on them until they are extended. If your pet is large, try this when it is standing next to you: With your leg, give the dog a slight push to the side, and it will resist your pressure (see HOW-TO: Winter Fitness, pages 58 and 59).

Worming and Vaccination

On walks, dogs easily pick up intestinal parasites that can weaken them considerably. In addition, infection with life-threatening

pathogens is possible even today. You can protect your pet from these dangers with regular
worming and annual inoculations.

Worming. A dog should first be wormed
while still a puppy, between the fourth and
sixth weeks of life. Then the treatment should
be repeated roughly every three weeks until
16 weeks of age. Your veterinarian can provide
you with appropriate medications to combat
roundworms, hookworms, heartworms, and
tapeworms. Since a stool sample is not always
clearly diagnostic of worm infestation,
preventive treatment makes good sense in
any case. Other intestinal parasites, too, can
cause symptoms similar to those of worm
infestation. Whenever worming proves

*While giving your pet its daily share of
stroking, you can ensure early detection
of health problems.*

unsuccessful, an examination by your veterinarian is indicated.

Signs of a possible worm infestation are
✔ loss of weight
✔ marked increase or decrease in appetite
✔ a bloated belly (don't confuse with baby fat)
✔ diarrhea
✔ an unkempt, dull coat
✔ coughing, exercise intolerance (heartworms)

Vaccinations. Only inoculation offers adequate protection against a number of life-
threatening infections. The cost incurred is

trivial, in comparison with the potential suffering. Vaccinations can be given to prevent distemper, parvovirus, hepatitis, parainfluenza, rabies, leptospirosis, coronavirus, kennel cough, and Lyme disease.

The first five vaccinations (core vaccines) should be administered to all dogs. The remaining four are optional, to be given at your veterinarian's discretion. Depending on the type of vaccination that is being given, booster immunizations of the core vaccines are normally given every three to four weeks until a puppy reaches 16 weeks of age.

For dogs over one year of age, consult your veterinarian for the ideal vaccination schedule. Many core vaccines may induce lifelong immunity; as a result, booster immunizations may not be necessary. The exception to this rule is the rabies vaccine, which needs to be given every one to three years, depending upon the law in your state.

Feeding Your Dog

A balanced diet tailored to your dog's individual needs is the basis for keeping it healthy and in good shape.

A healthful diet is a prerequisite for keeping your dog vigorous and fit.

Commercial Dog Food

Today, feeding a dog properly is no longer difficult. Stores offer a wide variety of canned and dry foods that contain all the vital nutrients, vitamins, and trace elements. Because dogs have a wide range of dietary requirements, depending on their age, level of activity, and state of health, there are many different food mixtures available, from puppy chow and food for seniors all the way to special products for canine athletes. Try them to see which ones your dog enjoys and digests well. Whether you feed your pet canned or dry food is your personal decision. With dry food, however, you need to make sure that your dog has plenty of water available.

As a rule, only dogs that engage in competitive sports in a club need special food, because they have an increased energy requirement. Normal food is completely adequate for a family pet, even if you exercise a great deal with it.

Food Additives

If your pet has certain preferences, you can add various foods to the commercial dog food. Make sure, however, that the commercial

product is nutritionally complete; that means that it contains everything a dog needs. If you mix in additional foods such as meat, rice, or potatoes, the result will be an imbalance in the composition of the diet. Adding some fruit, vegetables, and dairy products, however, will not be harmful.

Dairy products. Low-fat farmer cheese, natural yogurt, and cottage cheese, for example, will provide the dog with nutritionally valuable protein and calcium. Natural yogurt—that is, plain, unflavored yogurt—supplies the lactic acid bacteria important for digestion. You can give your pet dairy products daily. Pure milk, however, should never be fed to dogs. For puppies, nursing mothers, and convalescing dogs, special lactose-reduced products are commercially available, and they are easier for dogs to digest.

Fruit and vegetables. These will provide your dog with vitamins, minerals, and carbohydrates. Use this rule of thumb: Feed your pet in raw form only those fruits and vegetables that you would eat raw. Pure and unseasoned fruit and vegetable juices are also suitable additives.

Vegetable oils. Only cold-pressed products such as pumpkin oil, olive oil, and sunflower oil will supply your pet with essential fatty acids and vitamins. They will make its coat glossy and aid digestion. Three or four times a week, add—depending on your dog's size—$\frac{1}{2}$ to 1 teaspoon of cold-pressed vegetable oil to the food.

Feeding tricks. To make unfamiliar food, especially raw fruits and vegetables, more attractive, even to picky eaters, you can try using a few little tricks.

✔ Stir grated carrots or apples into the regular food to gradually get your pet used to the "new" taste.

✔ Rub fruits and vegetables with some meat or sausage (liverwurst, for example) or dip

TIP

Feeding Rules for Athletes

✔ It's not good to work out on a full stomach. Before athletic activity, always give your dog time to digest its food. Otherwise, especially with large breeds, there is a risk of life-threatening gastric torsion. The symptoms are a bloated upper abdomen, choking, and difficulty in breathing. The dog has to be taken to the veterinarian immediately, because such twisting of the stomach can lead to death in a few hours.

✔ After sports, too, let your pet rest before you feed it. Otherwise, eating is just an additional source of stress.

✔ Light snacks from a pet store are real treats that you can safely give your pet now and then, to increase its motivation. They should never replace a complete meal, however.

✔ For competitive athletes and for out-of-shape dogs, nutritional supplements can be used to boost the regular diet and purposely build up the animals.

✔ When your dog is active in sports, always keep an ample supply of fresh water available—especially in summer.

them in beef bouillon to make the taste more interesting to your dog.

Nutritional Supplements

A great many dietary supplements for dogs, designed for addition to normal food as flakes or pastes, are commercially available: vitamins, minerals, and trace elements to promote

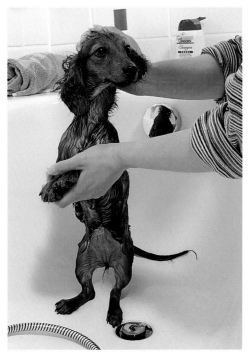

A bath cleans the coat and can also be helpful when a dog is shedding.

health; various additives that make a dog's coat glossy; and special preparations for senior dogs or puppies.

The need for such products depends greatly on your dog's state of health, its growth, and its activity level. Before feeding them to your pet, consult your veterinarian and discuss their use and the appropriate dosages. In certain situations and used with great deliberation, such products can be helpful in keeping your dog healthy or restoring it to health. For example, they can be used during the start-up phase of a training program, after serious illnesses, before or after operations, or during pregnancy

and nursing. The veterinarian can also provide you with concentrated nutrients, which, however, you should use only if your pet refuses to eat or is having health problems.

The Right Amount of Food

On the package labels of commercial dog food, you will find good guidelines for appropriate feeding. Since the caloric requirements of every dog are variable, you should check repeatedly to see whether your pet is getting the right amount of food. In a properly fed dog, the ribs are covered only by a thin layer of fat and can easily be felt. If you can no longer feel the ribs, more exercise and a fitness program are urgently needed.

Grooming Your Dog

Grooming, too, should be part of any fitness program. Only a dog that feels completely well can enjoy sports and games.

Regular Grooming Procedures

Coat care. You need a brush (available in pet stores). The amount of effort required depends primarily on the length of the dog's hair. For shorthaired breeds, brushing the coat once a week usually is sufficient. For longhaired dogs, as well as dogs that are shedding, this procedure has to be performed more often. Daily brushing is ideal. A thorough brushing not only removes dirt, but simultaneously massages the underlying tissue, thereby promoting good circulation. For breeds that need clipping, such as poodles and schnauzers, you also need the services of a professional groomer.

Nail care. Dogs that get enough exercise rarely have overgrown nails. If they are too long, however, they have to be trimmed, just like the dewclaws of certain breeds. For this purpose you need a special pair of clippers, available in pet stores. Have your veterinarian show you how to use them.

Grooming After Sports

A dog can get quite dirty hiking through fields and woods. Make it a rule to clean your pet's paws before you let it come indoors; that's easier than removing all the paw prints from your rugs and furniture after the fact. Don't forget to look for thorns or seed grains that may have become lodged in the paws.

Extremely dirty dogs need to be thoroughly brushed and—if they smell bad—given a bath. Don't forget to dry your pet well afterwards, to keep it from chilling. Dogs that aren't sufficiently toughened up also need to have their coats blow-dried, especially in winter. The long ears of breeds such as spaniels and Basset Hounds need special attention. They get dirty easily and should be cleaned after every walk. Keep in mind, too, that dirt, grass seeds, and insects may get into the outer ear canals and cause inflammation. If your dog holds its head at an angle or continually shakes its head and scratches, it may have such a problem. In such cases, you need to consult a veterinarian.

Parasite Control

If you spend a lot of time outdoors with your dog, it may well become infested with troublesome external parasites, especially from spring

By grooming their pet's coat, children learn how to correctly deal with the dog.

through fall. Remove all the little pests thoroughly, to keep your pet from suffering.

Fleas. When treating fleas on your dog, remember that collars, dips, and shampoos have little residual effect and are not useful for long-term control. Instead, use one of the new once-a-month flea control products available from your veterinarian. Keep in mind that these are different than the spot-on products available at pet stores, and work much better. Treating your home for fleas is best accomplished by sprinkling orthoboric acid powder on the carpets and near the baseboards of your home. This powder is easy to use, safe, and is readily available under various brand names from your local pet supply store.

Ticks. On your walks, try to avoid areas where your dog has a history of picking up

ticks. Certain spot-on flea products and flea sprays also offer some degree of protection against the annoying bloodsuckers. Ticks that are firmly lodged can be killed with a drop of oil and, after a few minutes, carefully removed with tick nippers (available in pet stores) or tweezers. Make sure that you remove the tick completely, including its head.

Mites are extremely small arachnids. Usually the only indication of a mite infestation in a dog is the persistent scratching that results. You can help by giving your pet a bath, using special medications available from your veterinarian. Your veterinarian can also administer a special oral medication designed to kill the mites.

For general prevention of external parasites, B vitamins and homeopathic remedies (sulfur D 30, given once a week during the danger season from spring to fall) are also effective.

Fitness for Puppies

A fitness program is important even for puppies, since the foundation for a dog's health, good behavior, and successful obedience training is laid while it is still a puppy.

Playing with Other Puppies

Puppies are born in a litter and grow up in a close community until the age of 12 weeks. While playing and tussling, they get the best kind of fitness training imaginable. When you bring such a puppy home, it naturally misses its littermates. Today, however, many obedience schools, dog sports clubs, and ASPCA groups offer play days for puppies, an opportunity that you definitely should take advantage of. Contact addresses are available from breeders' associations and the American Kennel Club (see Information, page 60). Through being with other dogs of its own age, a puppy not only gets the physical exercise necessary at this stage of life, but also learns the rules of canine

society in an enjoyable way. Shy animals gain self-confidence, and little tyrants are socialized by their peers.

Training Rules for Puppies

Games and fitness exercises are especially fun with puppies. Their clumsy movements make us laugh and awaken tender feelings. There are some things you need to bear in mind, however, when training a young dog.

Promoting self-confidence. Puppies need a high level of self-confidence to hold their own in daily life. Fitness exercises give a young dog a chance to encounter unfamiliar situations and cope with them successfully. Lavish your puppy with praise when it succeeds, especially if it is fearful and shy, but don't make too much of failures—you can even overlook some.

Don't overdo it. A young dog's body is not yet fully developed. If you ask too much of your pet, its bones and muscles can de damaged. Climbing stairs, running beside your bike, and jumping over hurdles are not suitable activities for puppies. Moreover, never let training or play sessions with your puppy last too long. Fifteen- to thirty-minute sessions four to five times a day are enough. If your puppy indicates that it is tired, stop and let it take a break. Like a baby, a young dog needs plenty of sleep so that it can develop properly.

Pointer. For a puppy, especially if it is still very young or belongs to a small breed, a walk often constitutes quite a substantial fitness program. Uneven patches of ground that you scarcely notice are a real obstacle course for a small creature.

Playing games helps puppies get fit and encourages good social behavior.

You're in charge: While playing with its human partner, a young dog learns to control its body, but it also finds out who's boss. Stick to the rules: What you allow during play, you can't prohibit once the game's over.

✔ If the play gets too rough, put your dog in its place with a friendly but firm "No."

✔ Don't give the puppy things to "play with" that are off limits the rest of the time, such as socks or a hand towel.

✔ Even in the most boisterous game, tables and seats should be taboo.

Important: Playing is no replacement for daily walks. A puppy also needs a chance to sniff around and to be with other dogs.

Great Games for Puppies

Tug of War. Take a soft toy that you can hold firmly, such as a cotton rag or a special tugging rope from a pet store, and move it back and forth in front of the puppy until it takes a bite. Then, start pulling on it, but carefully, so that you don't injure the little dog's sensitive milk teeth. The puppy, in turn, will start to tug, although it sometimes takes a while for it to get the idea of the game. Naturally, in reality it is you who determine the outcome of the competition. During the contest, you can show an aggressive, highly self-confident pup that you are the "leader of the pack." If your pet is shy and fearful, let it win more often, to boost its self-confidence.

Find it. Games involving searching and finding train not only the puppy's body, but also its powers of perception and sense of smell. Start by hiding a treat, to arouse the dog's interest in the game. While the puppy watches, conceal it under a newspaper or a cardboard box, and then order your pet to find it. Joining in the search yourself is the best stimulus for the puppy, which will try to find the treat before

you do. Don't forget to be lavish with your praise when your pet succeeds. Later, you can hide toys as well.

Races. Run a race with your puppy. At first, you'll be faster than it, but that will change over time. Make obedience training a part of your play: By talking to your pet and calling it, try to keep it running beside you at least part of the time. That way, it will learn to stay with you as you vary your speed on walks.

Fitness for Older Dogs

Older dogs, too, enjoy keeping fit. One positive side effect of the program: A carefully trained dog has a higher life expectancy, on the average.

Hiking is an ideal way to promote fitness, for young and old dogs alike.

When Your Pet Gets Older

Certain unmistakable, clearly visible signs will tell you that your dog is getting old:
✔ It clearly tires faster, and it needs more rest.
✔ In most breeds, the first gray hairs appear on the muzzle.

Simultaneously, internal signs of aging appear:
✔ Muscle mass decreases.
✔ The internal organs, heart, and circulatory system function less efficiently.
✔ Problems with the locomotor system appear (such as osteoarthritis or other painful conditions).

✔ Susceptibility to disease increases.

✔ The sensory organs function less efficiently.

The onset of this natural aging process also depends on the size of your dog: Small breeds begin to age only in their eighth year of life, on the average, while very large ones often start the process in their fifth year.

Training with Older Dogs

Exercise remains a basic need for older dogs as well. Even at a fairly advanced age, they are ready and eager to start a fitness program. Naturally, your pet's performance will progress at a slower pace. The training program should be carefully tailored to the dog's state of health. Discuss the options with your veterinarian.

Don't ask too much. In training, always bear in mind the dog's nature: It will follow its owner to the point of total exhaustion. It can be clearly overtaxed, and still run bravely at your side and wag its tail with joy when you speak to it. That can be very dangerous for older animals. You need to be extremely sensitive and observant where the length and intensiveness of your dog's training program are concerned.

✔ Walks that include easy exercises are especially good for older animals, since they can largely set the pace and have to exert themselves only for short periods of time.

✔ Between the exercises, take plenty of rest breaks.

With cardboard boxes, you can easily construct tunnels of various lengths.

✔ Games like Tug of War, Find it, or an easy obstacle course (see HOW-TO: Conditioning, pages 38 and 39) are suitable even for older dogs.

✔ With a well-trained senior, you also can continue your customary types of sports. Difficult exercises such as high jumps, however, should be discontinued over time, and the length of the session should be reduced.

Older dogs still need sensory stimuli. Many dog owners tend to let their less active older pet "just stay at their side" and thus unintentionally exclude the dog from their life, to a large extent. The dog is taken for granted as a kind of fixture and increasingly left behind and overlooked. In many cases, owners even acquire a second dog—as a rule, a lively puppy—that attracts the complete attention of the family. Especially for an older dog, however, it is crucial to be included in things: It needs sensory stimulation and plenty of encouragement if its final years are to be interesting and happy.

Fitness Calendar

	Spring (see page 33)	Summer (see page 40)
Sports and games	✔ Increase athletic activities to build up the dog's level of conditioning ✔ Take longer walks ✔ Swim in ponds and rivers (check water temperature) ✔ Increase time spent exercising in dog sports club ✔ Test dog's level of knowledge and obedience	✔ Shift walks and training to morning and evening hours, if possible ✔ On hot days, consider holding exercise sessions in your home ✔ Sports and vacation: swimming in lakes and ocean, playing on the beach, long hikes
Health	✔ Strengthen resistance through aromatherapy, Bach flower therapy, and homeopathy ✔ Watch for allergies ✔ Relax and build up muscles through massage and stretching ✔ Start worming treatments and begin heartworm prevention if indicated by your veterinarian ✔ Check to see whether shots are up to date	✔ Strengthen heart and circulatory system with aromatherapy and homeopathy ✔ Seek out shady spots to prevent heatstroke and sunburn ✔ Watch for allergies (such as summer dermatitis) ✔ Improve overall condition with hydrotherapy and massage
Nutrition	✔ Adjust diet to reflect increase in activity ✔ Use more supplementary foods: egg yolks, dairy products, and vegetable oils for skin and coat ✔ Start a course of vitamins ✔ Start to guard against possible overweight or underweight	✔ In hot weather, decrease food amounts ✔ Give your pet easily digestible food ✔ Use dairy products to supplement the diet ✔ Make sure the dog gets enough water
Grooming	✔ Brush more often (shedding season) ✔ Trim nails ✔ Check ears ✔ Get rid of parasites	✔ To protect from sun, apply sunscreen to areas with no pigmentation or where hair is sparse ✔ Possibly have thick-haired breeds clipped ✔ Check ears ✔ Get rid of parasites

Fitness Calendar

	Fall (see page 49)	Winter (see page 54)
Sports and games	✔ Intensify conditioning program ✔ Focus on preparing for exams in dog sports club ✔ Take extensive hikes through harvested fields ✔ Spend as much time as possible outdoors ✔ Swim in ponds and rivers (check water temperature)	✔ Cut back on conditioning program ✔ Adjust walks to weather ✔ Reduce training hours ✔ Do easy refresher exercises ✔ Move more fitness activities indoors ✔ Train the dog's senses through indoor play
Health	✔ Focus on strengthening resistance to colds through aromatherapy, Bach flower therapy, and homeopathy ✔ Do toughening-up work outdoors ✔ Watch for allergies ✔ Relax and build up muscles with massage and stretching ✔ Treat the dog for worms	✔ With aromatherapy and homeopathy, strengthen heart and circulation ✔ Preserve muscle development with massage and stretching ✔ Provide physical activity regularly, to prevent taut muscles ✔ Ward off colds with aromatherapy and use of homeopathic remedies
Nutrition	✔ Adjust diet to reflect increase in activity ✔ Increase amounts of supplemental foods ✔ Start a course of vitamins ✔ Add nutritional supplements (from pet stores) to the dog food ✔ Take steps to prevent possible overweight or underweight	✔ Reduce amounts of food to reflect decrease in activity ✔ Make sure the dog gets enough vitamins ✔ Add more dairy products to the diet ✔ Be sure you don't overfeed
Grooming	✔ Brush more often (shedding season) ✔ Check ears ✔ Get rid of parasites	✔ Brush coat regularly ✔ Trim nails ✔ Check paws for eczema caused by road salt

FITNESS IN SPRING AND SUMMER

The change of seasons offers you many ways to design a varied fitness program for your dog. Spring and summer are ideal times to start a training program and to gradually get your pet in good shape.

Plenty of Exercise in Spring

At last the low temperatures are a thing of the past. The weather again invites you to take lengthy walks that provide your pet with a host of new adventures. The dog will be overjoyed to go outdoors with you. It is especially important to give it a chance to play with other members of its species, so that its natural social behavior is retained.

Throughout spring and summer, most games and athletic activities take place outdoors. At these times of year, you and your dog will find special enjoyment in a fitness program. Dog obedience schools and clubs, too, will be offering increased opportunities for joint sports and conditioning. The range of offerings will be particularly wide near large towns; choose whatever most appeals to you and your pet. Take advantage of the opportunity to try something new, in order to develop the many different talents that are dormant in your pet and to keep its interest in physical exercise high.

Retrieving objects outdoors is a game that your dog will adore.

Fitness in Spring

Along with the rest of nature, our own spirits revive in spring. Now it's time to shake off the lethargy of winter and intensify your dog's fitness program again.

Sports and Games in Spring

Start with easy exercise, which you can gradually increase, however, until your dog is in top shape once more. The more you participate in the training, the more you and your pet will enjoy it. Fast runs across open country, retrieval of sticks or balls, and games of hide and seek are fun for every dog.

Biking with your dog. With the coming of spring, the season for bike rides also begins anew, and your dog is always glad to be included. Make sure, however, to carefully match your speed to your pet's condition and abilities. Small dogs, especially, are easily overtaxed on such outings. If possible, remove your pet's leash, so that it can set its own pace. That works only if the dog can be counted on to stay next to the bike, however. Pet stores offer special leash fixtures that are attached to a bike. Never tie the leash to the handlebars; that could cause an accident!

For longer trips with small dogs, you'll need a carrier basket.

Hiking with your dog. Hiking is good endurance training for both pet and owner. The steady, continual, but never overly strenuous activity helps get the dog in good shape without the risk of excessive strain. Whether in mountains or on flat terrain, there are plenty of attractive places to hike. To be safe, take along a supply of water for your dog, even if it usually finds places to drink outdoors. If you stop at an inn or restaurant, always request water for your pet. Generally, it will be provided free of charge.

Note: When hiking in the woods, always keep the dog on its leash. Even if it comes reliably when called on other occasions, its hunting instinct might prove stronger than the best obedience training.

Obstacle race. Every time you take a cross-country walk, you'll find plenty of obstacles to challenge both you and your dog. Have your pet jump across a ditch, or run up an earth bank or a steep hillside. The dog can crawl under benches along the roadside. Fallen tree trunks make ideal hurdles for your pet to clear. Along with your four-legged friend, you can practice balancing on large tree trunks. At first, put the dog on its leash and walk along beside the trunk. Once your pet can keep its balance, try the exercise without the leash. Special outdoor paths for physical fitness offer a host of interesting, exciting obstacles. Even in your own yard, you can set up a fitness course with a minimum of expense and effort (see HOW-TO: Conditioning, pages 38 and 39).

Caution: Never send your dog through pipes or across stacked tree trunks; it could be seriously injured.

Health in Springtime

In spring, you can do a great deal for your dog's health. Promote your pet's well-being, activate its energies, and don't forget to arrange for any preventive health care that is due, such as vaccinations, heartworm prevention, and worming treatments (see page 20).

Aromatherapy. Spring is a season of flowers and fresh scents. Now is the time to increase aromatherapy (see page 18), in order to stimulate your dog's body and soul. The following essential oils are especially appropriate at this time of year, to dispel spring fever and give your pet new energy:

Just being in a meadow is a huge adventure for a puppy. It can make a great many discoveries there.

✔ lavender (strengthening, healing)
✔ tangerine (balancing, relaxing)
✔ balm (calming)
✔ clary (strengthens circulation)
✔ orange (strengthening, restorative, refreshing)
✔ tea tree (healing, fights external parasites)
✔ lemon (refreshing, strengthening, restorative)

Aromatherapy is best used before you start your pet's training session, to give it the best possible preparation for physical exercise.

Bach flower therapy. Bach flowers (see page 18) can enhance your dog's senses, so that it can better perceive and process the abundance of sensations associated with spring. The combination of the individual flower essences, which is best left to an expert, depends on your pet's state of mind and its character.

These are especially recommended in spring:
✔ agrimony (strengthening, guards against excessive stress)
✔ centaury (restorative)
✔ olive (for exhaustion, restores inner balance)

For muscle cramps and minor injuries, the Bach Rescue Remedy ointment will help.

Homeopathy. With homeopathic remedies (see page 18), you can strengthen your dog's resistance, depleted by the winter, and help it develop a healthy coat and skin. These medications can also help get your dog fit again.

These active ingredients are especially important in spring:
✔ cinchona and echinacea, to strengthen general health
✔ sepia and sulfur, to promote healthy skin and a healthy coat

Massage and stretching. Speed up your dog's spring training and promote muscle development with massage (see page 19). That's the best way to get your dog ready for increased physical stress and to give it maximum protection against painful muscle cramping.

TIP

Vitamin Therapy

Vitamins are extremely important for health and performance, and in spring your dog needs an extra large helping of them: to get into good shape, to strengthen overall resistance, and to promote the shedding process. Especially in spring, make sure your pet has a vitamin-rich diet. Pet stores carry many different vitamin preparations. Before use, read the manufacturer's dosage instructions carefully. You can also add brewer's yeast flakes, as well as fruits and vegetables, to your dog's food (see page 23).

Note: Don't overdo it! An oversupply of vitamins, such as Vitamin A or D, can negatively affect your dog's health.

When stretching (see page 20), concentrate on the leg muscles, to strengthen them after winter's inactivity. Lay your dog on its side, and pull on each leg about 10 times, until the muscles are extended. Then repeat the entire exercise once more.

Feeding in Spring

To improve your dog's performance and restore its strength and vitality as quickly as possible, a balanced, healthful diet is especially important in spring (see page 22).

Food admixtures. To supply your pet with enough vitamins, minerals, and trace elements, you can mix one or two of the following ingredients in its food in alternation:
✔ 1 egg yolk (twice a week at most)
✔ 1 teaspoon of vegetable oil (see page 23)

✔ finely chopped green lettuce
✔ 1 raw carrot, grated
✔ 1 tablespoon of natural yogurt
✔ 1 tablespoon of sauerkraut juice.

Getting rid of extra pounds. Over the course of the winter, extra pounds can easily creep on because of insufficient exercise. A balanced weight-loss diet can help prevent that. Don't just reduce your pet's daily ration, however; instead, feed it low-calorie food mixtures. A wide selection of special diet foods is available in pet stores, as well.

Nevertheless, this applies to every reducing diet: If you want to lose weight, persistence is the most important thing. Light meat or fish broths with pureed vegetables, or natural yogurt

Skating with dogs is a quick way to get plenty of exercise—and to have plenty of fun, too.

with some lean chicken will calm your pet's growling stomach, especially in the first few days, without supplying an excess of calories.

While the spring diet is in force, follow these rules:
✔ Ensure that your dog always has fresh drinking water available.
✔ Make sure that the dog food is high in vitamins and minerals, to prevent symptoms of deficiencies.
✔ Don't revert to the customary diet until your pet really has lost weight and its condition has visibly improved.

Grooming in Spring

You need to devote special attention to your dog's grooming in spring.

Brush the coat carefully. Dry, heated indoor air during the winter and the natural shedding process have taken their toll. The dog's coat is dull, and the hair is coming out in clumps. For these reasons, coat care comes to the fore in springtime. At this time, all dogs need to be brushed frequently and thoroughly (see page 24). That is especially important for longhaired breeds, but a thorough brush massage is in order for shorthaired dogs as well, to improve the supply of blood to their skin.

Bathing the dog. If your pet's coat is in especially bad shape, or if the shedding process is slow, a bath is in order. This procedure will remove all the loose hair and improve the flow of blood in the dog's skin. Use a commercially available dog shampoo, to which you can add 1 teaspoon of olive oil, 1 teaspoon of aloe vera gel, and 2 to 4 drops of tea tree oil. That will benefit both coat and skin. If necessary, you can also use a special shampoo to control external parasites.

Cutting the nails. In winter, when walks tend to be fairly short, many dogs develop badly overgrown nails. They need to be trimmed (see page 24), to prevent injuries during sports and games.

Controlling parasites. With the approach of spring, pesky external parasites return as well. One sign that these pests are present: Your pet will scratch itself frequently or rub on various objects. Check your dog at least once a week for parasites such as ticks, fleas, or lice, and take countermeasures (see page 25) immediately if it is affected.

Checklist
Fitness in Spring

1 Examine the coat, skin, eyes, and ears for injuries, encrusted areas, and inflammations.

2 Check the dog's nails to see whether they need to be trimmed (see page 24).

3 Has your dog gained weight over the winter? If so, put it on a diet (see page 36).

4 Are vaccinations or booster shots (see page 20) needed? Is a heartworm check needed? Check your pet's veterinary record.

5 Worm your pet (see page 20).

6 Check your dog for external parasites (see page 25).

7 Determine your pet's fitness status (see TEST, page 11) before you start spring training.

8 For dogs with health problems, puppies, and older dogs, a checkup by the veterinarian is in order before you start a training program.

If your pet tires quickly, it will not only be unable to perform well, but also will be uninterested in performing well. Being in good physical condition is a basic prerequisite for being able to enjoy sports and games. In addition to plenty of spontaneous exercise on walks, which should last several hours, a special training program is an appropriate way to get your dog in better shape.

An Obstacle Course for Your Dog

Having your own obstacle course has many advantages:

✔ It can be closely tailored to your pet's size and talents.

✔ Training is not tied to the hours set by your dog sports club.

✔ In a nonstressful atmosphere, you can get your pet ready for training in the dog sports club and work on anxieties and problems at your leisure. There is room for an obstacle course in even the tiniest yard, and the course can easily be adapted to the space available.

An obstacle should always be just high enough for the dog to clear with ease.

An "economy model" can even be set up in your backyard.

Caution: Your dog can easily injure itself on sharp edges and on nails protruding from the obstacles; therefore, be sure none are present.

Suitable Obstacles

Hurdles can easily be made by placing broomsticks or fence slats on two stools of equal height. If the dog touches the obstacles, the bar should fall to the ground. Set it just high enough for your pet to barely clear with ease. Ideally, start with low obstacles and increase the height over the course of the training.

Tunnels are available in pet stores. Alternatively, you can make one simply by putting several cardboard boxes in a row. Take your dog's size into consideration, and don't build an overly long tunnel. The dog might get scared, and you should be able to get it out of the tunnel easily, if need be. At the outset, use a very short tunnel, and position yourself at the opposite end to call and beckon to your pet.

For a balance beam, you need a piece of wood about 6.5 feet (2 m) long and roughly 3.9 inches (10 cm) wide, laid across two large bricks or cinder blocks. Fasten it well at both ends, to keep it from falling when the dog tries to balance on top of it. Keep your pet on its leash until it masters the exercise.

For a slalom course, put broomsticks in the ground or set up plastic pails, placing the markers about 3 feet (1 m) apart and in a straight line. For this exercise, too, keep your pet on the leash until it understands what is expected of it.

The Sequence of the Obstacles

You can make the obstacle course a permanent fixture, or set it up again before each training session, creating new combinations as you choose.

While working on the balance beam, keep your dog on its leash, at least at the outset.

stores or supermarkets, you can erect a variety of obstacles easily and inexpensively. The size of the boxes is ideal, and they lend themselves to use in various combinations. Because of the different side lengths, the course can easily be adapted to your pet's size and physical condition. Give one of these obstacles a try:

✔ Place several boxes in a row, and let your dog balance on them.

✔ Use the boxes to build a wall for your pet to jump over.
✔ Using several boxes placed some distance apart, set up a series of hurdles.

Make sure to leave enough distance between the individual obstacles. After a jump, the dog needs enough space to get ready for the next obstacle. The length required between the obstacles depends primarily on the distance your pet can jump. If you have sufficient space available, you can also build a regulation obstacle course for one of the various types of canine sports.

A Course Made of Banana Boxes

Using banana boxes, which are available from fruit

By building an obstacle course yourself, you can incorporate as much variety as you like.

Playing in water is fun, as well as good exercise for muscles.

Fitness in Summer

Summer, with its long days and comparatively good weather, is the ideal time of year to get your dog into top shape.

Sports and Games in Summer

Because of the high temperatures, you need to place some restrictions on your pet's physical activities, to safeguard its health.

✔ Avoid physical exertion during the hot midday hours.

✔ Walks and athletic activities in the blazing sun should include generous breaks in shady spots.

✔ Make sure your pet gets plenty of water to drink.

Swimming alone or with you. Summer is the season for water sports—and for many dogs, swimming is a favorite activity anyway. Swimming and retrieving objects in the water are enjoyable ways of strengthening muscles without placing excessive strain on the locomotor system. To keep your pet healthy while it enjoys the swimming season, follow these rules:

✔ Make sure that the bank or shore has places where you can safely get into or out of the water.

✔ Avoid bodies of running water with a strong current or with high water levels; you may overtax your pet's abilities and place it in mortal danger.

✔ Motorboats and surfers, too, can endanger your dog.

✔ After being in the water, give your pet enough time to run around and dry off again. That will prevent chills and sore limbs. If your dog is sensitive, dry the external parts of its ears thoroughly.

✔ After being in salt water or mud, your pet should be rinsed thoroughly.

✔ Sand in your dog's coat can cause itching; after spending time at the beach, give your pet a good brushing.

Health in Summer

Health care in summer should take into account the dangers that extreme heat and allergies entail. Insect bites, too, can threaten your pet's health. You need to respond quickly (see page 42). In addition, you can use homeopathic methods such as Bach flower therapy or aromatherapy to improve the dog's overall state of health. Massage, stretching, and occasional hydrotherapy in a shallow body of water will round out your pet's health program.

Sunburn can affect dogs as well, especially in areas without pigmentation or where the coat is thin. Light-colored nose leather is especially susceptible. Light-skinned, shorthaired breeds such as Dalmatians can also get sunburned on their sides and abdomen. The symptoms are similar to those of humans, from reddening and scaling all the way to skin inflammation with a discharge. Generally, however, the skin that is

protected by the coat is less likely to be sunburned. Your veterinarian can recommend a sunscreen suitable for dogs. To ease the painful results of excessive exposure to the sun, try aloe vera gel, Bach Rescue Remedy ointment, and homeopathic ointments.

Circulatory collapse and heatstroke. The danger of circulatory collapse (shock) due to excessive heat is often underestimated in dogs. Even a brief stay in a closed, parked car in the hot sun can result in heatstroke and even in death. Physical exertion in high temperatures, too, can lead to serious problems.

If circulatory collapse is imminent, your pet will pant heavily, its eyes will roll, and it will begin to stagger. Get it to a shady spot at once. Use damp cloths to cool it down, and try to stabilize its circulation with suitable types of aromatherapy, Bach flower therapy, or homeopathic remedies. If your dog doesn't recover immediately, take it to the nearest veterinarian without delay.

Dogs, too, need a parasol for protection from sunburn and heatstroke.

TIP

Sports and Games on Hot Days

However wonderful summer may be, athletic activities during the middle of the day are stressful for your dog. Heatstroke or circulatory collapse can result (see page 41). If time constraints prevent you from moving exercise sessions to the early morning or late evening hours, you need to make some basic rules a part of your dog's training, to safeguard its health:

✔ Choose shady places at the edge of a wooded area or in a park.

✔ Let your pet take regular breaks.

✔ Stop the training session as soon as your pet starts to pant heavily.

✔ Don't let your pet exert itself for very long at a time. Several short training units are better than a single long one, in this case.

✔ Keep plenty of fresh water available.

Insect bites. Dogs love to snap at insects, and as a result they frequently are bitten on the mouth or jaw area. Where bees, wasps, or bumblebees are concerned, rapid first aid is called for, because the swelling sometimes can cause the dog to choke to death. Cool your pet's throat from the outside by placing ice cubes, a cold pack, or damp cloths on its neck. For internal cooling, offer your dog some ice cream this once. After these emergency measures, take your pet to the veterinarian without delay.

Insect bites on the dog's body can be treated with aloe vera gel or tea tree oil. That will reduce itching and largely prevent inflammation.

Allergies are especially common in summer. They can be caused by pollens, flea bites, flea-control products, insect bites, various other external parasites, sun, food, and many other things. One result can be summer dermatitis: weeping skin inflammations accompanied by hair loss. The inflamed areas are separated from the healthy skin by a distinct rim. These so-called hot spots can develop very quickly. Itching causes the dog to scratch and bite at these areas, and that makes the inflammation worse. Moreover, bacteria can penetrate and cause patches of eczema as broad as your palm. If that occurs, take your pet to the veterinarian immediately.

There are steps you can take to prevent summer dermatitis:

✔ Make consistent efforts to control fleas and other external parasites (see page 25).

✔ Longhaired dogs in particular need frequent brushing, to let air get to their skin (see page 24).

✔ For sensitive dogs, medicinal shampoos can help prevent skin problems. Consult your veterinarian.

Aromatherapy (see page 18) can stimulate appetite and stabilize circulation. These essential oils are especially appropriate in summer:

✔ basil (restorative, strengthens cardiac function)

✔ geranium (strengthening, cleansing)

✔ grapefruit (purifying, strengthening)

✔ tangerine (balancing, relaxing)

✔ clary (stimulates circulation, generally strengthening)

✔ neroli (encourages harmony, restorative)

✔ orange (strengthening, refreshing)

✔ tea tree (healing, strengthening, effective against external parasites)

✔ lemon (refreshing, strengthening)

During the hot part of the year, it is an especially good idea to use fresh herbs for aromatherapy. Place the selected plants in a vase near the place where your pet sleeps.

Bach flower therapy. Bach flowers, combined by an expert (see page 18), will stabilize your dog and help it better tolerate the summer heat. For circulatory problems of every kind (see page 41), give your pet Bach Rescue Remedy drops at once. For sunburn (see page 41), Bach Rescue Remedy ointment is a good form of first aid as well. These are especially appropriate in summer:

✔ chestnut bud (promotes ability to concentrate, strengthens perception)
✔ clematis (sustains interest in the surroundings)
✔ scleranthus (for emotional balance, gives inner strength and calm).

Homeopathic remedies (see page 18) will mobilize your dog's resistance to infection and help its circulatory system cope with the stress of summer heat. Sunburn will heal more quickly with the aid of homeopathic ointments (available in pharmacies). These active ingredients are especially important in summer:

✔ cinchona, echinacea, and mucosa, to improve the general state of health
✔ crataegus and veratrum, to strengthen and stabilize circulation.

Massage and stretching. Massaging your pet's chest and neck area (see page 19) will relax it, as well as activate and strengthen its circulatory system. Stretching (see page 20) will develop muscle structure without exerting your pet too much.

Hydrotherapy. Most dogs adore playing in the water. Take advantage of that, and do some hydrotherapy with your pet. Just let the dog run in shallow water, but for no more than 10 minutes. After an extensive break, however, you can repeat the exercise. That will strengthen its general condition, toughen it, and help get it in good shape. Suitable places for hydrotherapy are shallow streams and areas near the bank of ponds and lakes (see drawing, below). If you don't live near a convenient source of water, think about purchasing a child's swimming pool. Place it in a safe place, fill it with water, and allow your dog to exercise in it. A child's pool may not be ideal for exercise, but it will do in a pinch, especially for smaller dogs. Whatever water your dog exercises in, it should come about halfway up your pet's leg. Deeper water will make it too difficult for your dog to exercise easily.

Hydrotherapy in shallow water (see above) will improve your dog's general state of health.

Checklist
Fitness in Summer

1 If need be, have longhaired dogs with a thick, woolly coat clipped before the summer heat begins.

2 Examine your pet regularly for inflammations: They may indicate an allergy (see page 42).

3 With light-skinned dogs, take special precautions against sunburn (see page 41).

4 Does your dog have obvious circulatory problems (see page 41) on hot days? Take it to a veterinarian without fail.

5 Check closely for signs of external parasites: They can cause allergies.

6 Persistent lack of appetite may be due to something other than the heat. Consult a veterinarian.

7 Before any vacation trip, have your pet checked by a veterinarian.

Nutrition in Summer

Many dogs have less appetite in the summer heat, and digesting food seems too much work. Therefore, you need to follow these rules for feeding your pet:

✔ Meals should be especially light and easy to digest in this season, to keep from placing additional stress on your pet's body.

✔ Fresh foods will stimulate your pet's appetite, too. Add natural yogurt, vegetables, and fruit to its diet.

✔ In summer, feed the dog early in the morning, if possible, or in the evening.

✔ In this season, make sure that the dog is drinking enough fresh water. If it generally drinks little, add a little moisture to its meals.

Grooming in Summer

As a rule, your dog will need little grooming in summer. Just pay close attention to external parasites, since this is high season for the little pests. Examine the dog regularly for skin parasites (see page 25), and take steps immediately to control any you may find. Bear in mind that fleas are the primary cause of allergies and the dreaded summer dermatitis (see page 42).

Short haircut for summer. Dogs with thick hair suffer especially in the summer heat. To help your pet get through the season more comfortably, it's a good idea to have its coat clipped by a professional groomer. With a little less hair, the dog will be happier and fitter throughout the summer.

Note: As an alternate to the above, if you have a thick-coated dog, instead of clipping it, you could use a slicker brush and a comb with long, wide-spaced teeth in your regular grooming sessions. By doing this, you will be removing a large amount of the undercoat,

which will ventilate the skin and make the dog more comfortable. It will also protect the skin from direct sun and the unwanted attention of biting insects. Sometimes clipping the outer coat may create a whole new set of problems for a dog in the summer.

Grooming supplies. The following is a list of grooming supplies that should help you keep your dog in good condition in the summer:
✔ rake
✔ slicker
✔ wide-tooth comb
✔ flea comb.

Getting Rid of Summer Odors. Dogs often come into contact with skunks during the summer. If your dog meets one of these cute but

To the dog's delight, children will gladly take over part of the fitness program.

smelly creatures head on, the following are two remedies for removing the skunk's lingering, musky odor from its coat.

1. One good remedy for removing skunk odor is to wash your dog with tomato juice and then give it a bath using dog shampoo and water. Rinse your dog off with water and lemon juice or vinegar.

2. You can also try a pet-safe odor neutralizer that can be used to bathe your dog. Read the directions carefully to make certain that the product can be used to bathe your dog.

A training program is not always easy to implement in a city, but even there, with a little skill, you can find a quiet spot for exercise or games without disturbing anyone.

On vacation, however, working on fitness is easy, virtually automatic, as a rule. There are a great many opportunities for physical exercise, depending on the location in which you decide to spend the nicest weeks of your year.

Physical Exercise in Town

Avoiding obstacles: Benches, trash receptacles, and lampposts make perfect obstacles. With your dog, run at a fast pace, zigzagging around the objects. After some time, your dog will be able to perform such exercises without your help (see drawing, page 47).

Running across obstacles: Even in a park, you can construct a small obstacle course with rocks and branches that you find on the ground. The purpose of the exercise is for the dog to raise its legs really high as it runs, without having to jump long distances as well. The height of the obstacles, of course, depends on the dog's size. In any event, the animal should be able to negotiate the obstacles without any real problems. Don't forget to dismantle the course when you're done.

Playing ball and Frisbee: Ball games are a way to really get your pet moving. Large open areas in parks are especially good for games that involve throwing, which are good training for a dog's endurance and ability to sprint. In addition to balls, Frisbees are good for games of this kind: You can throw them a long way, and some dogs develop acrobatic abilities as they try to catch them.

Inline skating with your dog: With inline skates, you're much faster than you are on foot, and you can ask more of a pet that accompanies you. Accidents, however, can easily occur. If possible, remove your pet's leash.

Tip: Many dogs will have great fun on a skateboard. Put the dog on the board, and push it around to get it accustomed to moving in this way. Once the dog starts to enjoy itself, you can give the board a more vigorous push. Be careful, however; don't let the dog get hurt.

Jogging: If you own a medium to large breed of dog, jogging is an excellent

Dogs love to play Frisbee. There are plenty of opportunities for a game when you go swimming.

You can use lampposts as markers in an urban slalom course.

way to improve your dog's physical condition, as well as your own. Especially in the early morning hours when the city is still quiet, it's fun to run with your pet on sidewalks, through pedestrian zones, or through parks. Make sure that at least some portion of your route is not covered with asphalt, however; otherwise, the dog's feet could get sore.

If necessary, you can put your pet on its leash for jogging. If you do so, the dog needs to keep even with you at all times, and the leash should not be taut.

Physical Exercise on Vacation

Vacationing at the beach: The beach is an ideal fitness course. Running in the soft sand is excellent exercise for muscles, and a beach covered with fine sand offers dogs a perfect opportunity to get their fill of digging for once. Some animals are real masters at building sandcastles, and such activity is a good way to strengthen the muscles of the front legs and chest. Bury a toy in the sand to get your dog interested in digging.

Frisbees, balls, or pieces of wood are good exercise equipment at the beach. Depending on your pet's talent, you can try throwing these objects into the water, as well as along the beach, and then have the dog retrieve them. Getting family members, partners, or friends involved in the training is a great way to promote fitness. Throw the ball or the Frisbee back and forth. Your dog will do its utmost to catch the object. Now and then, let it succeed; otherwise, it will lose interest quickly.

Vacationing in the mountains: The dog's physical condition will be strengthened on long hikes, and there will be plenty of opportunities for negotiating obstacles. In dangerous areas, however, always put your pet on its leash. If the dog is very small, take along a fabric sling, so that you can carry it if it runs out of steam. During your stay, pay a visit to the local dog club, where you'll have a chance to become familiar with different training methods.

On a long mountain hike, don't forget water for your dog.

FITNESS IN FALL AND WINTER

The cold season is announcing its approach, but that's no reason for a dog owner to hole up next to a warm stove with his or her pet. On the contrary: To keep your dog healthy throughout these months, getting it in good shape now is especially important.

Getting Ready for Winter

Fall and winter can be a difficult time for your dog. Only too often, the customary walks have to be cut short. The consequence: Both owner and pet get too little exercise. It's precisely at this time, however, that the dog's body needs all its strength to stay healthy through the months ahead. The foundation for health has already been laid in an active spring and summer. Build on it now by turning the training program up a notch, until your pet is in top shape. Because of the often-unreliable weather, however, you'll probably need to move part of the exercises into your home.

In fall and winter, keep an especially close eye on health issues. Especially in wet, cold weather, your dog's immune system can be stressed. After walks in the rain and outdoor training sessions, you need to ensure that your pet is clean and dry. A really fit animal, however, can manage even the nastiest weather.

Even without sports equipment, there are plenty of opportunities to be physically active.

Fitness in Fall

Despite the dropping temperatures, there are still nice days in fall that you can use for training outdoors.

Sports and Games in Fall

Walking in fallen leaves. A lengthy walk in fall offers your dog numerous opportunities to play. It simply can't resist the appeal of the rustling leaves. Toys are especially easy to hide—and fun to hunt for—at this time of year. Every pile of leaves invites your pet to jump in. Because of the strange, intense smells, the dog will wallow and burrow with abandon. Let it romp to its heart's content.

Hiking. Fall, pleasantly cool after the summer heat, is the season for extensive hikes. Ideally, plan day-long trips with your dog; they will both boost and stabilize its level of fitness. Such hikes are especially enjoyable in the company of other dog owners. A well-planned day trip in a beautiful natural setting is an unforgettable experience for owner and pet alike.

In fall, you need to deliberately get your dog ready for the long winter months. Increase the training requirements to an even higher level, to improve fitness and build muscle. Slowly get your pet accustomed to the worsening weather, now damp and chilly. If you both are tough and hardy, you and your dog will be less susceptible to illness, and you can look ahead to winter without concern.

Braving the Elements

A healthy dog with a well-developed coat can stand even wet, cold weather. To toughen your pet, give it an opportunity to be outdoors in bad weather for an extended period (several hours) on a regular basis. It won't hurt the dog to get soaked on occasion. Just make sure you always dry it thoroughly afterwards, without delay.

Increasing Endurance

Your dog's physical condition and ability to perform—like your own—do not remain at a constant level, but are subject to fluctuation. There are numerous reasons for that: The dog's state of health, its living conditions, and, not least, the seasons of the year have an influence. In winter, for example, performance and fitness drop, just as the rhythm of life slows. Therefore, you need to boost your pet's physical condition to a high level in fall.

The best method for that is regular endurance training, with your dog covering fairly long distances at moderate speed with you as you bike and jog. That way, your pet will not only get used to the increasingly cool, wet weather, but also reach peak condition quickly.

Set a High Standard

Someday, let your pet show what it's capable of: Exercise the dog until it's really "out of steam" and its exhaustion is obvious. That will be a good opportunity for you to gauge its level of fitness, and the dog, too, usually will welcome the challenge.

If your pet can't sustain a high level of performance for even a short time, then you need to further intensify its training program until winter arrives. There is still time to intervene successfully. After any exertion, however, your dog needs a fairly long break, so that it can recover completely.

Toughening Up Sensitive Dogs

Some dogs, like some humans, are

Walking through a field after the harvest makes muscles strong.

Running Across Stubble

Grain fields—once harvesting is finished—or freshly plowed fields are an ideal place for an obstacle course with a high degree of difficulty. Running across stubble or furrows is strenuous for a dog, but it is a great way of exercising its muscles.

YOUR PET

Wet, cold autumn weather doesn't bother a dog that is sturdy and tough.

Aromatherapy in Fall

The following mixtures of essential oils are especially good for building up your pet's resistance, as well as your own.

The oil mixtures are used in a scent lamp. You can make a larger quantity if you wish: Use five drops of each oil, and keep the mixture in a dark bottle in a cool place.

To strengthen resistance:
1 drop geranium oil
1 drop tangerine oil
1 drop clary oil
1 drop neroli oil

To ward off illness:
1 drop eucalyptus oil
1 drop fennel oil
1 drop chamomile oil
1 drop sage oil
1 drop orange oil

especially sensitive individuals; they catch every germ that comes around, and they tire quickly. Such dogs have to be handled with special consideration if they are to perform well, and they have to get in shape gradually. To toughen them and improve their endurance, try walks that include easy athletic activities, swimming, and hikes.

To run beside a bike without a leash, a dog needs to have had good obedience training.

Competitive sports. In fall, many dog sports clubs hold competitive events that are meant to reward the hard work and effort of spring and summer with exams and trophies. Even if the success you seek is not forthcoming, that's no reason to give up. Your dog may just have had a bad day, or the competition may have been simply too good this time. Don't let a failure diminish your affection for your pet, however. Keep your dog healthy throughout the winter, and try again next year. Your four-legged friend's motivation—like a human's—may fluctuate. If your pet doesn't seem to enjoy the exercises, try taking a break from the training program for a while. If the drop in motivation lasts too long, however, it's time for

Dogs that become accustomed to horses early on can be taken along when you ride.

a checkup by the veterinarian. Sore limbs or an illness could be the cause.

Health in Fall

Fall can entail health problems for your dog: Wet, chilly weather can stress the immune system. Here, you need to react immediately, using appropriate countermeasures such as aromatherapy or homeopathic remedies, so that any symptoms of illness are brought under control and disappear quickly. If symptoms persist, or a cough or fever is present, consult a veterinarian.

For older dogs with osteoarthritis or aching limbs, the complaints increase as the temperatures drop. Then you need to protect your pet as well as possible against cold and damp, and on especially dreary days, move the training sessions indoors.

The tougher your dog is (see HOW-TO: Toughening Your Pet, pages 50 and 51), the sturdier its health should prove in this difficult time of year.

Aromatherapy. Fall is the right season for full-bodied, strong aromas with a strengthening effect. On a regular basis, put a scent lamp (see page 18) near the place where your pet sleeps.

The following oils are especially suitable in fall; often they will stop minor illnesses before they can really get started:
✔ eucalyptus (strengthening)
✔ fennel (balancing)
✔ chamomile (strengthening)
✔ lavender (healing, strengthening, helps control external parasites)
✔ tea tree (healing, strengthening)

Bach flower therapy. In fall, too, Bach flowers (see page 18) can aid your dog. Especially good during this season are balancing flower essences, which will help your dog deal with the changes that autumn entails.
✔ cerato (promotes self-confidence)
✔ gentian (gives self-confidence and strength)
✔ vervain (balancing, gives energy)

Follow this rule here as well: The combination of the individual flower essences depends on your pet's emotional state and should be determined by an expert.

Homeopathy (see page 18) is especially helpful in fall. Appropriate medications promote overall health and ease the discomforts of sore limbs and other maladies. These active ingredients are especially important in fall:

Checklist
Fitness in Fall

1 Check the dog's skin very carefully for inflammations: They interfere with the growth of the winter coat.

2 Parasites appear again in large numbers. Before winter comes, worm your dog (see page 20), and get all parasites under control (see page 25).

3 Test your dog's level of fitness before stepping up the intensity of the fall training program (see TEST, page 11).

4 Remove any hard seeds between the pads of your dog's paws—they can cause inflammation.

5 Make sure your dog has had all its shots (see page 20).

6 If your dog, despite the training of the past few months, still tires quickly and pants heavily, consult your veterinarian. The dog may have heart disease, a thyroid disorder, or other malady.

Parasite Control

In fall, parasites reappear in quantity. Fleas, lice, ticks, and mites appear in large numbers. The number of commercially available products for parasite control is equally large. Products with long-lasting action have proven successful in combating fleas, lice, and ticks (see page 25). They eliminate the bother of powdering and bathing, and they also replace the flea collar. Application is easy, and the dog is protected on all its walks. Remember, however, that very sensitive dogs may have an allergic reaction to these products. If in doubt, consult your veterinarian without fail.

Mites can cause itching and a variety of skin changes. Usually only a veterinarian can determine whether these tiny pests are present.

Intestinal parasites are a danger all year long. Thoroughly worming your dog before winter will improve its general health and help it get through the cold months with greater ease.

✔ cinchona and echinacea to improve overall health
✔ sepia and sulfur for skin and coat
✔ hepar sulfuris, luffa, and pulsatilla to ease the discomfort of illness
✔ dulcamara to combat rheumatism.

Massage and stretching. When you intensify the training program in fall, massage (see page 19) can be very helpful. It strengthens muscles, aids circulation, and relaxes the entire body. For dogs with back and hip problems, massage the affected areas with great care and regularity, to stimulate muscle development.

Stretching exercises (see page 20), too, especially involving the back and hip areas, can have long-term benefit.

Nutrition in Fall

As training intensifies and the heat diminishes, you need to slowly make your dog's meals more substantial, so that it can build up the cushion of energy required for the winter. If you feed your pet commercial dog food, enrich it with egg yolk twice a week. Vitamin preparations, too, can be added in larger quantities.

Those measures also assist the approaching shedding process, which consumes a great deal of the dog's energy. Make sure, however, that you don't overdo things; your dog should not gain an excessive amount of weight at this time.

Grooming in Fall

Shedding. In fall, your dog has to be brushed more frequently once again because it will lose plenty of hair during the shedding process. A bath will get rid of most of the loose hairs.

Controlling parasites. Don't forget about the need for parasite control in fall. Since the little pests can survive the winter in a warm house, you need to examine your dog thoroughly and combat any parasites systematically (see TIP, left).

Fitness in Winter

Winter, too, offers ample opportunity to stay active and fit. Go outdoors with your dog on a frequent basis; that will help it get through the long hours indoors more successfully.

Sports and Games in Winter

Winter sports with a dog have a charm all their own. Sledding or walking in crisp, cold weather is an exceptional experience for both owner and pet. In addition, most dogs enjoy nothing more than a lively snowball fight. And even when the weather is really terrible, there still are plenty of opportunities for indoor training (see HOW-TO: Winter Fitness, pages 58 and 59).

When planning winter activities, keep these guidelines in mind:

✔ Don't let your pet swim outdoors; its wet coat will freeze.

✔ Curtail the dog's training if the snow is very deep and the temperature is extremely low.

✔ For dogs, trips to an ice rink always entail a high risk of injury.

Important: When you're out in the cold, keep moving at all times; otherwise, your pet's muscles will stiffen and be prone to injury.

Health in Winter

If your pet has been put through a good training program the rest of the year, it will have few health problems in winter. Now the focus should be on strengthening resistance, to keep viruses and bacteria from gaining a foothold.

Aromatherapy. In winter, a season with a natural dearth of scents, aromatherapy is especially valuable (see page 18). It provides both owner and pet with a reminder of the smells they will encounter again in spring, summer, and fall. Also, emotional balance, an active circulatory system, and good resistance are particularly important at this time of year.

In winter, these oils are especially suitable:

✔ eucalyptus (strengthening)

✔ fennel (balancing)

✔ geranium (strengthening, cleansing)

✔ chamomile (strengthening)

✔ mimosa (emotionally restorative, strengthening)

✔ neroli (harmonizing, restorative)

✔ tea tree (healing, strengthening, combats parasites)

✔ vanilla (calming, balancing)

✔ cinnamon (calming, relaxing, warming).

*Playing in the snow with
another dog is especially nice.*

Checklist
Fitness in Winter

1 Did shedding take place in due order? If your pet is still shedding in winter, ask a veterinarian for advice.

2 Apply butterfat to your dog's paws to protect them from the salt on streets and sidewalks, which irritates the skin.

3 Check the dog's weight regularly. Avoid excessive weight gain during the winter.

4 Senior dogs are more apt to suffer from aching limbs now. Keep your pet especially warm and dry.

5 Look for pressure sores due to long periods spent lying down—they can become inflamed. Try to offer your pet something softer to lie on.

The warm scents of Christmas spread a feeling of coziness and warmth—something that dogs enjoy as well.

Bach flower therapy. Winter does have its rigors: Darkness, bad weather, and chilly temperatures can certainly dampen the spirits of owner and pet alike. Depression is common at this time of year, even in an otherwise lively dog. To combat such moods, try carefully selected Bach flower drops (see page 18). They will stabilize the dog's emotional state and help your pet stay cheerful and full of vitality during the dark months of the year.

The following essences are especially helpful at this season:
✔ clematis (keeps the dog interested in its surroundings)
✔ honeysuckle (increases zest)
✔ hornbeam (promotes liveliness and mental alertness)

Homeopathy. In winter, there is a greater need to strengthen resistance and thus overall health. Especially helpful in that effort are homeopathic remedies (see page 18). Minor illnesses and bouts of pain caused by osteoarthritis, for example, can be successfully treated with such remedies.

The following active ingredients are especially important in winter:
✔ cinchona, echinacea, and mucosa to improve general health
✔ dulcamara to combat rheumatism
✔ hepar sulfuris and pulsatilla.

Massage and stretching. In winter, many dogs lie listlessly in the house, spending hours in the same spot. Painful muscle tension is the result. Here, gentle, thorough massage (see page 19) can bring noticeable relief and also stimulate circulation. Spoil your pet in this way at least once a week. And don't forget to do

stretching exercises with the dog regularly (see HOW-TO: Winter Fitness, pages 58 and 59).

Nutrition in Winter

Since our dogs today live primarily in houses or apartments, there is no need for a "high-nutrition diet" in winter. It will only make the dog overweight, and you'll have to work hard with your pet to get the extra pounds off again in spring. A normal, healthful, vitamin-enriched diet is completely adequate in most cases.

Grooming in Winter

Coat care. Brushing should be part of the regular weekly grooming routine in winter. It

You can use games involving mental exercise to train your pet's five senses. Try hiding a little treat, for example.

stimulates the blood supply to the dog's skin and promotes the growth of its new coat.

Paws. Pay special attention to the care of your pet's paws now. Road salt irritates the skin and can cause inflammation. As a preventive, rub butterfat or Vaseline between the pads of the dog's paws.

If salt nevertheless gets on your dog's paws be sure to wash it off completely as soon as you notice it. Otherwise, it could become a serious problem for your dog.

Even if it proves difficult to go outdoors in winter, don't let your pet's fitness program suffer. Depending on the weather, you can play winter sports with the dog or hold a training session indoors.

Repeating Lessons Indoors

Many commands that have been learned outdoors can easily be practiced indoors as well. A positive side effect: The dog will get exercise and build muscle. Don't restrict yourself to just the simple commands "Sit," "Down," and "Come." Every home has room for jumping over a box or a broomstick. With a sheet, stitched together, and two frames cut from a cardboard box, you can make a little tunnel that your dog will love to crawl through. There are virtually no limits upon your imagination when it comes to devising games. Just keep one thing in mind: Never use items that are part of the regular furnishings for the training session; otherwise, your dog will eagerly use them as an obstacle course in your absence as well.

Stretching

Stretching exercises (see page 19) are a perfect way to build muscle gently and lastingly during winter training

Training Your Dog's Senses

Take advantage of winter to train your pet's five senses at home:

✔ From another room, call your pet in a low voice. That will test its hearing, sharpen its alertness, and involve it more closely in your daily life.

✔ Holding a toy at different heights, move it back and forth in front of your pet. The dog will follow the object with its eyes and thus train its eye muscles and ability to focus.

✔ While your pet is sound asleep, carefully lay a treat in front of its nose. Some dogs will react immediately,

Winter is a good time to train your dog's sense organs.

while others need more time. This method can also tell you which scents get more of a reaction from your pet.

indoors. They can be done almost anywhere in your home, without special equipment. Concentrate on your pet's legs, which usually don't get enough exercise in winter, when walks are curtailed. The neck and back muscles, too, need some attention.

Cross-country Skiing with Your Dog

Take your pet with you when you go cross-country skiing; it is a perfect form of endurance training. The dog

can easily run along the cross-country course without its leash. Since the pace is not rapid, it will also have ample opportunity to sniff and to cultivate social contacts. In wooded areas, however, always keep the dog on its leash unless you are certain that it won't seek to gratify its hunting instinct.

Snowball Fights with Your Dog

Dogs are real ball artists, always in the mood for a

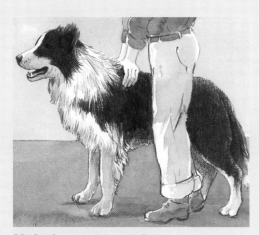

Ideal indoor training: stretching.

should wear its leash, unless you're certain that it won't run away.

Sledding with Your Dog

It's best to take the whole family along when you go sledding with your dog—it will be even more fun. As you sled, the dog will run around you in circles, barking happily, and race downhill after you. It's an ideal opportunity to let it play freely in the snow. Some dogs even enjoy coasting downhill together with their owner. Large dogs can even pull the sled, provided their health permits it. For that, you need a harness, so that you can successfully transfer the dog's pulling power to the sled. Make sure you choose a level area for this activity, however. Going uphill is far too strenuous, and going downhill the sled might travel faster than the dog, which could cause injury.

good snowball fight. Make a loose snowball, and simply toss it up in the air. Your dog, with acrobatic leaps, will try to catch it before it hits the ground. In fact, your pet will willingly play any game at all, as long as it can run around in the soft snow. If your dog eats snow, it is advisable to use a regular ball or some other toy, instead of a snowball. Otherwise, gastrointestinal problems could result.

Hiking in the Snow

Hiking across the snowy countryside can be a peaceful, serene experience for both owner and pet. Choose fields or woods that other humans seldom visit. You'll be more likely to see interesting things there. In winter, many animals are out and about during the daytime hours, and dogs are very interested in their relatives living in the wild. Here, too, your pet

Sledding is fun for owner and pet alike.

Associations
American Humane Association
9725 East Hampton Avenue
Denver, CO 80231

American Kennel Club
260 Madison Avenue
New York, NY 10016
Web site: http://www.AKC.org
For Registration, Records, Litter
Information:
5580 Centerview Drive
Raleigh, NC 27606

American Veterinary Medical
Association
930 North Meacham Road
Schaumburg, IL 60173

Canadian Kennel Club
111 Eglington Avenue
Toronto 12, ON
Canada

Books
Alderton, David. *Dogs.* New York:
    DK Publishing Company, 1993.
American Animal Hospital
    Association. *Encyclopedia of
    Dog Health and Care.* New
    York: The Philip Lief Group,
    Inc., 1994.
American Kennel Club. *The
    Complete Dog Book.* New York:
    Macmillan Publishing
    Company, 1992.
Animal Medical Center. *The
    Complete Book of Dog Health.*
    New York: Howell Book House,
    1985.
Coile, Caroline D. *Encyclopedia of
    Dog Breeds.* Hauppauge:
    Barron's Educational Series,
    Inc., 1998.

Periodicals
AKC Gazette
51 Madison Avenue
New York, NY 10010

Dog Fancy Magazine
P.O. Box 53264
Boulder, CO 80322-3264

Dog World
29 North Wacker Drive
Chicago, IL 60606

Gaines Touring with Towser
P.O. Box 5700
Kankakee, IL 60902

About the Author
Linda Waniorek has been a dog
owner for many years, and her
expertise is based on long experience. For over 15 years, she has
been deeply committed to the
prevention of cruelty to animals,
and she continues to find new
homes for older dogs and cats.

About the Photographer
The photos in this book are the
work of Christine Steimer. A free-
lance photographer since 1985,
she has specialized in animal
photography since 1989.

About the Illustrator
György Jankovics, a graphic artist,
studied at art academies in
Budapest and Hamburg. He draws
animals and plants for a number
of well-respected publishing
houses.

Acknowledgments
The publisher wishes to thank Dr.
Uwe Streitferdt, a Munich veterinarian specializing in small-
animal medicine, for his critical
review of the material on
preventive health care.

Photos:
Page 1: Agility—a type of
canine sport that is available in
clubs.
Pages 2 and 3: Retrieving
objects in water is an ideal way
to keep in shape.
Pages 4 and 5: Catching a
Frisbee also teaches the dog to
jump.
Pages 6 and 7: Jump ropes are
excellent for Tug of War.
Pages 64 and 65: Playing in
shallow water is fun for a dog,
as well as good training for its
muscles.

I N D E X

After the training session comes a well-earned break.

Important Note

This book gives advice to the reader about caring for a dog. The author and publisher consider it important to point out that the advice given in this book applies to normally developed puppies or adult dogs, obtained from recognized breeders or adoption shelters, dogs that have been examined and are in excellent health with good temperament.

Anyone who adopts a grown dog should be aware that it has already formed its basic knowledge of humans. The owner should watch the dog carefully, especially its attitude and behavior toward humans. If possible, the owner should meet the former owner before adopting the dog. If the dog is adopted from a shelter, the owner should make an effort to obtain information about the dog's background, personality, and peculiarities.

Caution is further advised in the association of children with dogs, both puppies and adults, and in meeting other dogs.

Well-behaved and carefully supervised dogs may nevertheless cause damage to someone else's property or cause accidents. It is therefore in the owner's interest to be adequately insured against such eventualities, and we strongly urge all dog owners to purchase liability policies that cover their dogs.

English-language translation copyright © 2001 by Barron's Educational Series, Inc.

Original title of the book in German is Fitnessplaner für den Hund.

Copyright © 2000 by Gräfe und Unzer Verlag GmbH, Munich, Germany.

Translation from the German by Kathleen Luft.

All inquiries should be addressed to:
Barron's Educational Series, Inc.
250 Wireless Boulevard
Hauppauge, NY 11788
http://www.barronseduc.com

Library of Congress Catalog Card No. 00-054675

International Standard Book No. 0-7641-1873-0

Library of Congress Cataloging-in-Publication Data
Waniorek, Linda.
    [Fitnessplaner für den Hund. English]
    Fitness planner for your dog / Linda Waniorek; [translation from the German by Kathleen Luft].
        p. cm.
    Includes bibliographical references (p.).
    ISBN 0-7641-1873-0 (alk. paper)
    1. Dogs. 2. Dogs—Health. 3. Dogs—Exercise. I. Title.

SF427.W2613   2001
636.7'08937—dc21   00-054675

Printed in Hong Kong
9 8 7 6 5 4 3 2 1

1 When can I start working on my puppy's physical fitness?

You can start when the puppy is 8 to 12 weeks old, but make sure you don't overdo it (see *Fitness for Puppies*, page 26).

2 Can older dogs take part in a fitness program, too?

Older dogs in particular should be in good physical condition—that will increase their life expectancy.

3 What if my dog is physically impaired?

A fitness program can do a lot to balance out physical impairments. Let your veterinarian help design the program.

4 Which breeds are suited for dog sports?

Dog sports and fitness training are suitable for every breed. Keep in mind the typical abilities of your pet's breed, however.

5 Will a special diet help keep my pet fit?

Every dog needs a healthful, well-balanced diet. Therefore, no special diet is necessary in a fitness program. Only competitive athletes need special foods.

Our expert answers the 10 most frequently asked questions about physical fitness programs for dogs.